PIRACY

Lynn Peppas

Crabtree Publishing Company

www.crabtreebooks.com

Crabtree Publishing Company

www.crabtreebooks.com

Author: Lynn Peppas

Publishing plan research and development:
Sean Charlebois, Reagan Miller
Crabtree Publishing Company

Photo research: Rachel Minay, Lynn Peppas

Editors: Rachel Minay, Kathy Middleton

Proofreader: Crystal Sikkens

Design: Tim Mayer (Mayer Media)

Cover design: Ken Wright

Production coordinator and prepress technician: Ken Wright

Print coordinator: Katherine Berti

Produced for Crabtree Publishing by
White-Thomson Publishing

Photographs:
Alamy: Mike Goldwater: title page; North Wind Picture Archives: pp. 6–7; **Associated Press**: Farah Abdi Warsameh: front cover; **Corbis**: pp. 28–29; Badri Media/epa: pp. 18–19, Eric Thayer/Reuters: pp. 32–33; HO/Reuters: pp. 12–13; Michael S. Yamashita: pp 26–27; partha sarkar/Xinhua Press: pp. 3, 42–43; Peter Turnley: pp. 40–41; **Getty Images**: Getty Bloomberg: pp. 14–15; **Press Association**: Elizabeth Williams/AP pp. 38–39; Farah Abdi Warsameh/AP: pp. 1, 22–23; **P–Trap from Westmark bv**: pp. 44–45; **Shutterstock**: DVARG: back cover; ChameleonsEye: p. 9; **White-Thomson Publishing/Stefan Chabluk**: pp. 8–9; **Wikimedia**: pp. 4–5, 10–11, 16–17, 20–21, 24–25, 30, 31, 36, 36–37; www.sealswcc.com: pp. 34–35.

Disclaimer: Wherever possible, images from the *Maersk Alabama* incident have been used in this book. Where no suitable images were available, other images have been used to tell the story.

Library and Archives Canada Cataloguing in Publication

Peppas, Lynn
    Piracy / Lynn Peppas.

 (Crabtree chrome)
Includes index.
Issued also in electronic formats.
ISBN 978-0-7787-1103-2 (bound).--ISBN 978-0-7787-1123-0 (pbk.)

    1. Maersk Alabama (Ship)--Juvenile literature. 2. Hijacking of ships--Somalia--Juvenile literature. 3. Piracy--History--Juvenile literature. I. Title. II. Series: Crabtree chrome

HV6433.786.S58P47 2013   j364.16'4   C2012-908193-0

Library of Congress Cataloging-in-Publication Data

Peppas, Lynn.
 Piracy / Lynn Peppas.
   pages cm. -- (Crabtree chrome)
 Includes index.
 ISBN 978-0-7787-1103-2 (reinforced library binding : alk. paper) -- ISBN 978-0-7787-1123-0 (pbk. : alk. paper) -- ISBN 978-1-4271-9245-5 (electronic pdf) -- ISBN 978-1-4271-9169-4 (electronic html)
 1. Piracy--Somalia--21st century--Juvenile literature. 2. Maersk Alabama (Ship)--Juvenile literature. 3. Piracy--History--Juvenile literature. I. Title.

 DT403.2.P47 2013
 364.16'4--dc23

                                        2012047915

Crabtree Publishing Company

Printed in Canada/012013/MA20121217

www.crabtreebooks.com   1-800-387-7650

Published in Canada
Crabtree Publishing
616 Welland Ave.
St. Catharines, ON
L2M 5V6

Published in the United States
Crabtree Publishing
PMB 59051
350 Fifth Avenue, 59th Floor
New York, New York 10118

Published in the United Kingdom
Crabtree Publishing
Maritime House
Basin Road North, Hove
BN41 1WR

Published in Australia
Crabtree Publishing
3 Charles Street
Coburg North
VIC 3058

Contents

Criminals at Sea

Lookout for Pirates

Crew members on the American **cargo** ship, *Maersk Alabama*, were on the lookout for pirates as they sailed the Indian Ocean near the coast of Somalia, in Africa. On April 8, 2009, they spotted a small boat quickly speeding toward them. Their greatest fear—a pirate attack—was about to happen.

▼ *Cargo ships such as the* Maersk Alabama *carry cargo to different ports around the world.*

Criminals of the Sea

Pirates are dangerous criminals that commit crimes at sea. Modern-day pirates work for large, criminal groups who work from land. They attack all kinds of ships for money. They steal, take people prisoner, and even kill.

In the first nine months of 2012, pirates attacked over 200 ships around the world.

cargo: goods carried on a vehicle such as a ship

Thousands of years ago, pirates stole a ship's cargo of treasure. Pirates made more money by selling the crew as slaves. Piracy was most common from about 1650 to 1725. Sometimes pirates attacked ships and forced the sailors to become pirates, too.

▲ *This 19th-century illustration shows a merchant ship (a cargo or trade ship) being attacked by Chinese pirates.*

Pirates today demand a **ransom** for the safe return of the ship and people onboard. They often do not steal cargo because they cannot sell it in poor countries such as Somalia. Ships are worth millions of dollars. People's lives are priceless.

Pirates from long ago often lived aboard ships for months—sometimes years—at a time.

ransom: the price paid for the safe return of a person or item

Modern-Day Pirates

Modern-day pirates do not live at sea on large ships for long periods of time. They use small speedboats with large motors so they can travel quickly. These fast boats help them catch larger ships.

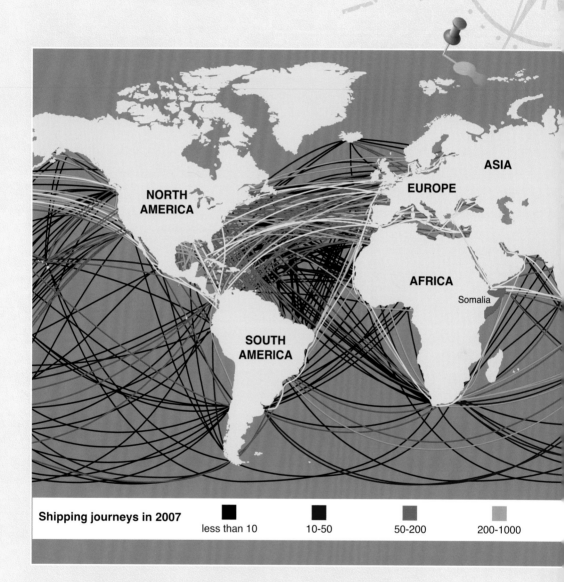

Shipping journeys in 2007

| less than 10 | 10-50 | 50-200 | 200-1000 |

▲ *This map shows major* **shipping routes**. *The dark red lines show the fewest journeys along these routes (the least-traveled routes); the light yellow lines show the most journeys (the most-traveled routes). Modern-day pirates attack ships in popular shipping routes near countries that do not guard the water along their coasts.*

Pirate Attack

Unlike pirates of long ago, who raised black flags to show they were attacking, modern pirates sneak onboard at night. Sometimes they make threats first by radio or fire gunshots at the ship. There is no chance for surrender.

AUSTRALIA

1000-5000   more than 5000

Most modern-day pirates work off the coast of Asia, Africa, South America, and parts of North America such as the Caribbean.

▼ *In the past, skeletons were sometimes used to decorate pirate flags. The "skull and crossbones" put fear into the hearts of many sailors.*

shipping routes: sea lanes regularly used by merchant ships

Pirate Attack!

Pirate Warning

On April 7, 2009, the *Maersk Alabama* was carrying **aid** to Kenya, a country in Africa that was suffering a food shortage. Sailors onboard were watching out for pirates. Pirates had radioed the ship earlier, demanding the ship stop. The captain, Richard Phillips, decided to speed up and try to outrun them. The ship was able to escape—this time.

▶ *Pirates often use large, stolen fishing boats as mother ships.*

The Mother Ship

Pirates work from a larger, main ship, called the mother ship. It is used as their command center. Pirates send smaller, faster speedboats called skiffs from the mother ship to attack big cargo ships such as the *Maersk Alabama*.

> "Now there were two other fast boats back there, plus a larger [ship] following eight to nine miles behind us ... The mother ship ... was trailing us."
>
> *Maersk Alabama* Captain Richard Phillips

mother ship

skiff

aid: something given to help or support others who need it

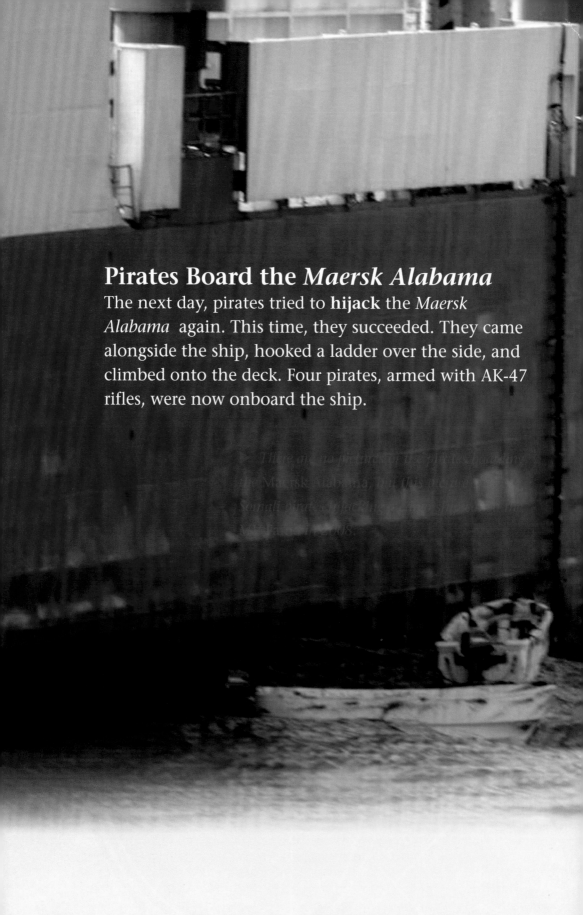

Pirates Board the *Maersk Alabama*

The next day, pirates tried to **hijack** the *Maersk Alabama* again. This time, they succeeded. They came alongside the ship, hooked a ladder over the side, and climbed onto the deck. Four pirates, armed with AK-47 rifles, were now onboard the ship.

Easier Target?

Newer cargo ships are built smaller and faster. They need fewer sailors to operate them. Having fewer sailors onboard is good news for pirates. This means they have fewer people to worry about during a hijacking.

Anti-piracy training teaches sailors what to do in case of a pirate attack. Sailors onboard the *Maersk Alabama* knew exactly what to do.

hijack: to take control of a vehicle such as a ship or aircraft

Captured Captain

Prepared for the Worst

Sailors heard the alarm. Most ran to the ship's safe room and locked themselves inside. Pirates captured Captain Phillips and two sailors on the **bridge** of the ship. Pirates held guns to their heads and demanded they gather the others.

▲ A ship's bridge holds important equipment that steers the ship, shows the location of the ship and others close by, and provides communication throughout the ship and with the outside world.

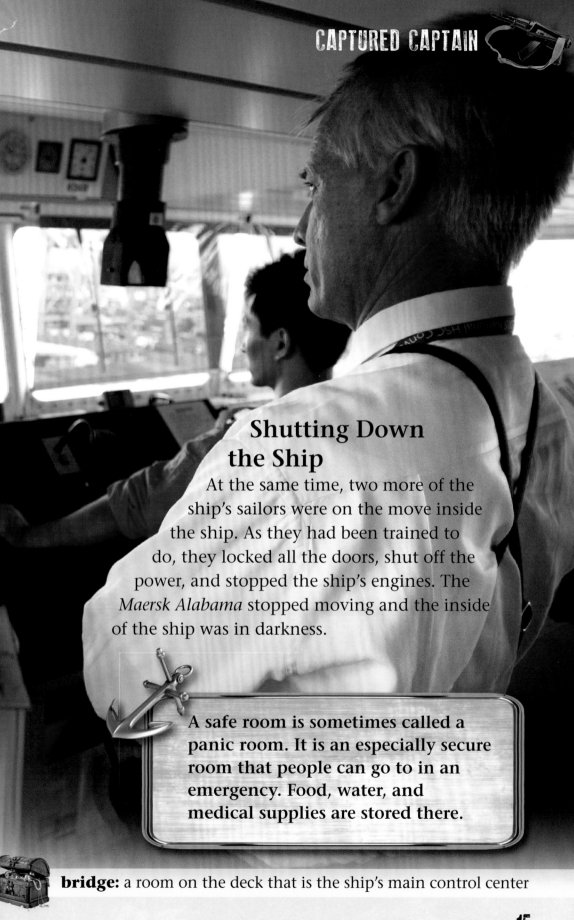

Shutting Down the Ship

At the same time, two more of the ship's sailors were on the move inside the ship. As they had been trained to do, they locked all the doors, shut off the power, and stopped the ship's engines. The *Maersk Alabama* stopped moving and the inside of the ship was in darkness.

A safe room is sometimes called a panic room. It is an especially secure room that people can go to in an emergency. Food, water, and medical supplies are stored there.

bridge: a room on the deck that is the ship's main control center

Dangerous Game of Hide and Seek

Pirates forced the captain, at gunpoint, to call the crew. But the pirates did not know that there was a secret password. The captain called, but did not use the password. The crew knew it was not safe to come out.

Pirate Targets

Pirates target many different kinds of boats. They capture large oil tankers, cargo ships, fishing boats, and small yachts. Pirates take over the ship and sometimes **kidnap** the people onboard. They hold ships and people for ransom and will not release them until they are paid.

"If a ship is from [North America] or [has] valuable cargo like oil, [or] weapons ... then it's like winning a lottery jackpot. We begin asking a high price ..."

A Somali pirate

SIRIUS STAR

◄ *Oil tankers carry millions of dollars in oil.*

kidnap: to capture a person and hold them against their will

Capturing the Pirate Leader

The chief engineer of the *Maersk Alabama*, Mike Perry, bravely waited in the dark for the pirates. His only weapon was his pocketknife. Perry heard a pirate coming and attacked him. It was the pirates' leader, Abduwali Abdukhadir Musi. Perry injured Musi during the fight and captured him.

Armed and Dangerous

Perry was lucky that the pirate leader, Musi, was not carrying his AK-47 when he attacked Perry. Modern-day pirates carry modern weapons such as machine guns and rocket-propelled **grenades**.

◄ *Pirates carry destructive weapons that can do a lot of damage to ships and harm crew members.*

American-owned ships do not allow weapons onboard. They tell sailors to not fight back so they won't risk getting hurt or killed.

grenades: containers filled with explosives

Hostage Situation

The pirates on the bridge held the *Maersk Alabama's* captain **hostage**. Two sailors below held the pirate leader hostage. One of the sailors got on the ship's intercom. He wanted to make a deal with the pirates to trade hostages.

Let's Make a Deal!

In exchange for their captain, the sailor offered the pirates the return of their leader, Musi. He also offered a lifeboat to escape in and $30,000 in U.S. cash. The pirates agreed to the deal. The sailors set the pirate leader free.

◀ *Hostages live in fear that they will be murdered at any time. This picture shows the crew of the hijacked MV Faina standing on the ship's deck.*

"They said they would shoot someone if their friend [Musi] did not come back. For me, that was the toughest moment."

Chief Officer Shane Murphy

hostage: a person who is held against their will

▶ *Pirates often wait onshore for ransoms to be paid.*

Money or Your Life

The pirates took Captain Phillips with them to the lifeboat. They made him get in to show the pirates how to work the boat. However, the pirates did not let the captain go as they had promised. They decided to keep him and demand a ransom for his life instead.

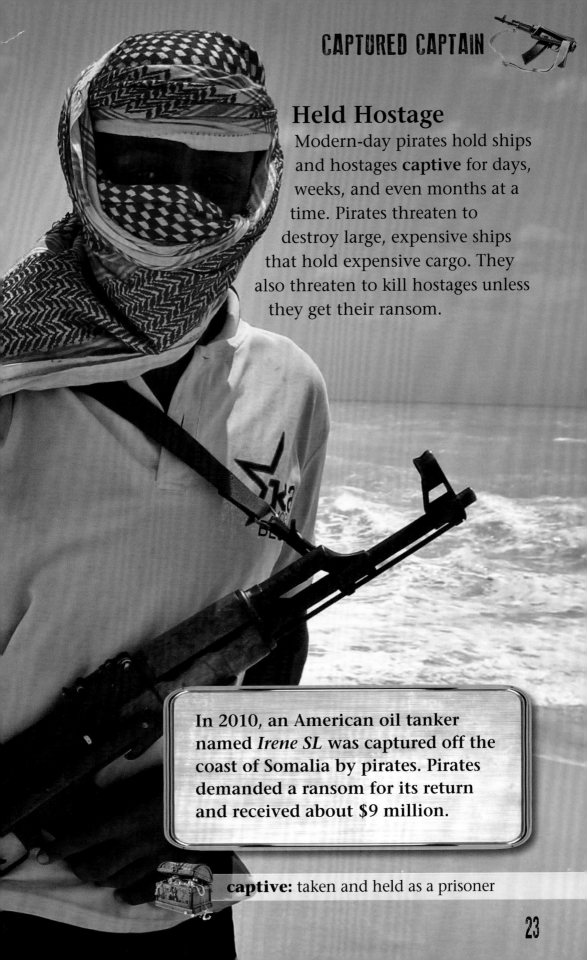

Held Hostage

Modern-day pirates hold ships and hostages **captive** for days, weeks, and even months at a time. Pirates threaten to destroy large, expensive ships that hold expensive cargo. They also threaten to kill hostages unless they get their ransom.

In 2010, an American oil tanker named *Irene SL* was captured off the coast of Somalia by pirates. Pirates demanded a ransom for its return and received about $9 million.

captive: taken and held as a prisoner

USS *Bainbridge* to the Rescue

A U.S. Navy **warship** called the USS *Bainbridge* came to rescue the *Maersk Alabama* the next day. USS *Bainbridge* carries two Sea Hawk fighter helicopters, missiles, and guns. Americans were prepared to do battle to get the captain back.

▶ *Warships such as the USS* Bainbridge *have the most modern weapons onboard.*

Attempt to Escape

The captain waited for a chance to jump off the lifeboat when the pirates were not watching. During his first night on the lifeboat, he escaped by diving into the water. He swam toward the USS *Bainbridge*, but the pirates caught him before he reached it.

"I knew there were sharks off the coast of Somalia [but] ... if anything was going to kill me that night, it was the pirates."

Captain Richard Phillips

warship: a navy's ship that is armed for combat

Captured, Again

The pirates were angry with the captain for trying to escape. They beat and tied the captain up. They used a two-way radio to talk to military men aboard the USS *Bainbridge*. They wanted a $2 million ransom for the captain's life.

▲ *Pirates threaten to destroy ships and kill people to get the ransom they want.*

To Pay or Not to Pay

American commercial ship owners, or their **insurance companies**, usually do pay the ransom in these situations. Sometimes, relatives of the hostages pay the ransom for the release of people held on private yachts. For the *Maersk Alabama*, the U.S. military decided not to pay a ransom for Captain Phillips. They sent in the Navy SEALs instead.

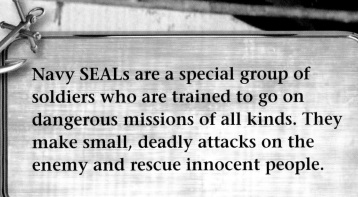

Navy SEALs are a special group of soldiers who are trained to go on dangerous missions of all kinds. They make small, deadly attacks on the enemy and rescue innocent people.

insurance companies: companies that pay for damage or loss

Help from Above

Navy SEALs are a specially trained U.S. military force that works on land, sea, or in the air. The SEALs secretly **HALO jumped** at night from an aircraft into the sea near the USS *Bainbridge*. A boat from the warship picked them up and brought them onboard.

▶ *HALO stands for "high altitude, low opening." When Navy SEALs HALO jump, they only open the parachute at the very last moment.*

Snipers Ready

Three Navy SEAL snipers hid at the back of the USS *Bainbridge*. Snipers are excellent shots. They can shoot with great accuracy from far away. Each sniper kept his eyes and his gun on the pirates.

> "[The SEALS] step off the steel and into the dark. All they hear is the wind whistling past them ... Then ... they're in the water."
>
> Kevin Dockery, SEAL expert

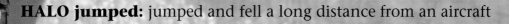

HALO jumped: jumped and fell a long distance from an aircraft

Stop That Lifeboat

The lifeboat was heading for the shore of Somalia. Land was only about 24 miles (39 kilometers) away. If the pirates got the captain onto land, he might disappear with them forever.

▲ *One of the warships that helped with the rescue was USS Halyburton, a guided missile frigate. USS Halyburton sprayed water from fire hoses to push back the lifeboat.*

How to Stop a Pirate

The U.S. Navy wanted to stop the lifeboat from reaching shore. Other warships arrived to help. Sea Hawk helicopters hovered overhead and created **hurricane**-like winds that also held the lifeboat back. The pirates fought back with gunfire.

Pirates held the captain hostage on the small lifeboat for over three days. It was completely enclosed, hot inside, and without a toilet.

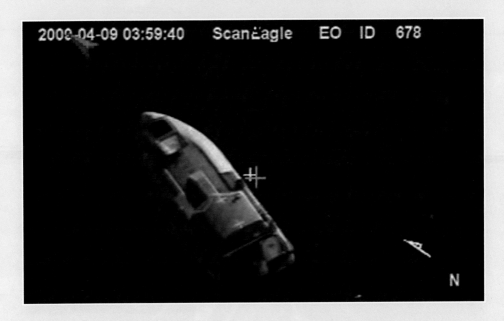

2009-04-09 03:59:40   ScanEagle   EO   ID   678

N

▲ *The Navy used an aerial vehicle called ScanEagle to track the lifeboat. The SEALs worried that if the pirates got the captain to land they would never find him alive.*

hurricane: a storm with winds greater than 73 mph (117 km/h)

Desperate Times

The pirates were growing more desperate. The lifeboat was running out of fuel and food. Musi, the pirate leader, had injured his arm in the earlier fight on the *Maersk Alabama*, and the injury was getting infected. The pirates sent a radio message to the Navy, demanding supplies.

◀ Musi was taken to the USS Bainbridge to have the cuts on his hand treated. Surrendering to U.S. troops saved his life.

Pirate Leader Surrenders

The Navy brought supplies in a rubber boat. They tied a **cable** to the lifeboat from the USS *Bainbridge* and promised to tow the pirates to the Somali shore. Musi left with a Navy SEAL to be treated by a doctor. Now there were only three pirates left with the captain.

The pirates believed the USS *Bainbridge* was pulling them to shore. In fact, they were slowly pulling the lifeboat closer to the warship.

cable: a strong wire rope or metal chains

Finger on the Trigger

Each of the three Navy SEAL snipers had one pirate
he had to keep his eyes and gun on. The Navy
decided to kill the pirates to
save the captain's life.

Shoot to Kill

The snipers waited patiently for their order to shoot. It was difficult because the lifeboat and ship were moving up and down on the waves of the Indian Ocean. **Night-vision scopes** attached to their guns helped them see their targets during the pitch-black night.

◀ *Snipers are trained to hit targets from far away.*

"This is what [Navy SEALs] train for. If those snipers don't feel they can hit the target they won't pull the trigger."

Kevin Dockery, SEAL expert

night-vision scopes: gun attachments that help the user see at night

Ready, Aim, Fire

To succeed, the snipers would have to shoot all three pirates at the same time. They also had to make sure they did not hit Captain Phillips. If even one of them missed their target, the captain would likely be killed.

▲ *Following his dramatic rescue, Captain Richard Phillips (right) shakes hands with Frank Castellano, the commanding officer of USS* Bainbridge.

Deadly Success

The snipers had only one chance. Each Navy SEAL had his target in his sights. When the opportunity came, they all fired together. All three pirates were hit. The captain was not hurt in the gunfire. The military **operation** came to a successful end.

> "I share the country's admiration for the bravery of Captain Phillips ... His courage is a model for all Americans."
>
> U.S. President Barack Obama

◀ *After being held hostage for almost five days in the tiny lifeboat, Captain Phillips was rescued by the U.S. Navy.*

operation: the organized actions of a military or navy force

Pirate Charged

The only pirate to survive was the leader, Musi, who had surrendered earlier. He was taken to the United States, jailed in New York City, and charged in three different pirate attacks.

▶ *The Somali pirate leader was just 18 years old when he committed his crimes. He will spend most of his life in jail in the United States.*

Jail Time

Musi was charged with piracy and other **offenses** such as hostage-taking, kidnapping, hijacking, and planning to harm a ship and its crew. He pleaded guilty in February 2011 and was sentenced to almost 34 years in jail.

Somali pirate Abduwali Abdukhadir Musi is serving time at the Federal Correctional Complex in Terre Haute, Indiana.

offenses: wrongdoings or crimes

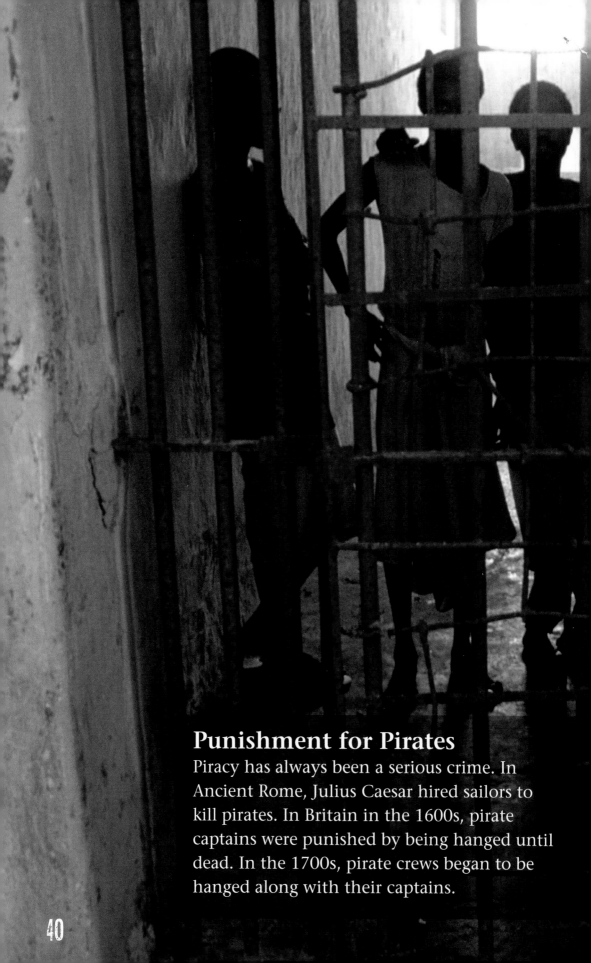

Punishment for Pirates

Piracy has always been a serious crime. In Ancient Rome, Julius Caesar hired sailors to kill pirates. In Britain in the 1600s, pirate captains were punished by being hanged until dead. In the 1700s, pirate crews began to be hanged along with their captains.

Modern-Day Punishment

International laws have been passed by the United Nations (UN) organization to control piracy. Still, different countries have different laws. In the United States, piracy is punished by life in jail. In Somalia, pirates get a life sentence, too, although many are released early to make room for other criminals coming in.

The United States had not tried anyone as a pirate for almost 100 years before Abduwali Abjukhadir Musi was charged with the crime.

◀ *In Somalia, many pirates receive life sentences, but are released early because Somali prisons are too full.*

international: all around the world

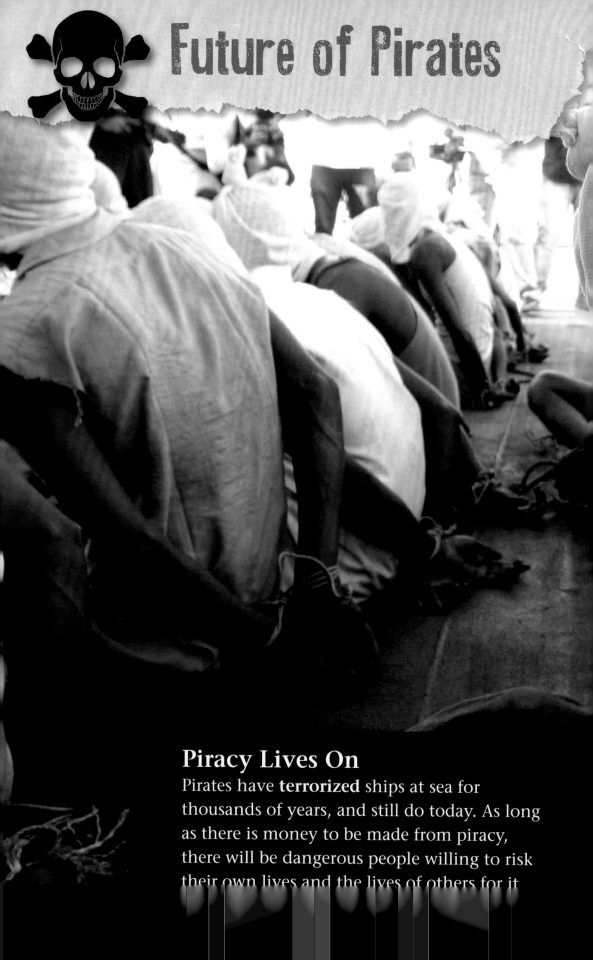

Future of Pirates

Piracy Lives On

Pirates have **terrorized** ships at sea for thousands of years, and still do today. As long as there is money to be made from piracy, there will be dangerous people willing to risk their own lives and the lives of others for it

Taking the Risk

There are more pirates from Somalia than from any other country. Somalia is a desperately poor nation and many young men turn to crime. When pirates don't get caught, they make a lot of money. When they do get caught, they pay with long jail terms.

◀ *These suspected Somali pirates were captured in the Indian Ocean in 2011.*

In 2011, a total of about $160 million in ransoms were paid to pirates from Somalia.

terrorized: overpowered and filled with fear and distress

Fighting Against Piracy

Ship owners are trying to keep a step ahead of pirates. They hire armed **security** teams to protect their ships. Ships are being built that have better security equipment and can travel at faster speeds to outrun pirates. Ships also try to stay away from shipping routes known for pirate attacks.

New Technology

Ship owners also use new technology in the fight against piracy. The P-trap—"P" stands for pirate—makes it harder for pirates to board a ship. Bars attached to the ship drag lines beside and behind the ship just below the surface of the water. These lines stop a motorboat from coming alongside a ship to board.

"The key to [a pirate's] success is that [pirates] are willing to die, and the crews are not."

A Somali pirate

security: the state of being safe

Learning More

Books

In The News: Modern-Day Piracy
by Jason Porterfiled
(Rosen Publishing Group,
2011)

A Captain's Duty
by Richard Phillips and
Stephan Talty
(Hyperion, 2010)

Kidnapping and Piracy
by John Humphries
(Franklin Watts, 2011)

Websites

*www.thekidswindow.co.uk/
News/History_Of_Pirates*
History of pirates

*http://people.howstuffworks.com/
pirate5.htm*
Modern-day pirates

*http://news.nationalgeographic
.com/news/2006/07/060706-
modern-pirates.html*
A National Geographic news
article

Movies/ Documentaries

*Somali Pirate Takedown:
The Real Story*
Discovery Channel
Docudrama. Can be viewed at:
*www.maritimetraining.com/
Product/Somali-Pirate-
Takedown-The-Real-Story*

Glossary

aid Something given to help or support others who need it

bridge A room on the deck that is the ship's main control center

cable A strong wire rope or metal chains

captive Taken and held as a prisoner

cargo Goods carried on a vehicle such as a ship

grenades Containers filled with explosives

HALO jumped Jumped and fell a long distance from an aircraft

hijack To take control of a vehicle such as a ship or aircraft

hostage A person who is held against their will

hurricane A storm with winds greater than 73 mph (117 km/h)

insurance companies Companies that pay for damage or loss

international All around the world

kidnap To capture a person and hold them against their will

night-vision scopes Gun attachments that help the user see at night

offenses Wrongdoings or crimes

operation The organized actions of a military or navy force

ransom The price paid for the safe return of a person or item

security The state of being safe

shipping routes Sea lanes regularly used by merchant ships

terrorized Overpowered and filled with fear and distress

warship A navy's ship that is armed for combat

Index

Entries in **bold** refer to pictures